STEPHA

MW01616729

HOW TO TALK TO

Guys

Everything you
need to cover in
the *first* four dates

How To Talk To Guys
Everything You Need To Cover In The First Four Dates
By Stephanie May Wilson

RELIGION / Christian Life / Love & Marriage

ISBN: 978-1-7348715-2-4

Design by Luum Studio
HelloLuum.com

Printed in the United States of America

Remember: You are worthy of love
—*today, and always.*

INTRODUCTION

The rom coms make it look so easy: Guy meets girl. Guy asks girl out. And they live happily ever after. But that's never been my experience. Here are three scenarios that feel a little more realistic to me, and maybe you can relate to them too:

Your best friend decides to set you up with her cousin. She talks him up endlessly and tells you all the reasons you're perfect for each other. Finally, she gives him your number and a few days later, he texts you. You try not to get your hopes up too high, but the truth is you have all the hope in the world. Isn't this how all great love stories begin? You can picture it unfolding perfectly.

As you start to text him back, you realize you're not sure what to say (or how to say it!). You want to get to know him and you want to make a great impression but doing those things via text is so hard!

Or maybe the scenario looks more like this . . .

There's this guy at church who you've had a crush on for what feels like forever. He's a great guy, and you find yourself scanning the crowd at church for him more than you'd like to admit. The problem is you haven't had the chance to get to know each other.

You chat occasionally, but every time you do, you find yourself hopelessly tongue-tied. You want to say something smart, funny, and charming. You want to get to know him and to let him get to know you, but you just cannot figure out a way to make that happen.

How do you go from, "Would you please pass the creamer?" at the coffee bar to having a great conversation that ends in him asking you out on a date? You have no idea.

So, there you are, asking for the half-and-half, feeling defeated, and promising yourself, *I'll try to talk to him again next week.*

Or maybe you fall into the third scenario when you decide to try online dating. You match with a guy who seems cute and who appears to have some common interests with you. He messages you, or maybe you message him, and it starts out okay. You introduce yourself and make small talk, you ask some questions and he asks a few in return. But then you hit a wall, and you wonder, *What am I supposed to say next?*

Somehow you're supposed to carry on a conversation with a total stranger that's going to tell you all of the information you need to know in order to decide if he's a good fit for you. Do you have things in common? Do you share the same faith? And, at a bare minimum, should you try to meet up in person?

And on top of that, you're also trying to be funny, smart, attractive, and stand out from every other girl on the dating website—all at the same time.

Is anyone good at all of that?

Friend, if your brain turns to mush and elephants stampede around in your stomach (we're *way* past butterflies at this point!) when you think about these scenarios, know that you are *so* not alone.

I consider myself a confident woman. I've always been social and I'm comfortable speaking in front of large groups of people. Even so, just the memory of talking to a guy I liked is enough to make me queasy. (And this is coming from a woman who's been married for several years!)

So, hear me: You aren't bad at this. It's hard and totally daunting... unless you have a plan. And that's exactly what you're holding in your hands right now.

In this book, you'll find a script of conversation-starting questions that will make all of these scenarios so much easier. And bonus, they'll help you stand out from the crowd and keep your conversations flowing effortlessly as you get to know the guy you're talking to. No matter the scenario, these questions will empower you to feel calm and confident through those crucial initial conversations.

HOW TO START A CONVERSATION WITH A GUY

It's one thing to carry on a conversation once you're already in the midst of one, but how do you start something out of thin air? If you run into a cute guy on an app, at a coffee shop, or at church, how do you strike up a conversation? What do you say?

STEP 1: IF YOU WANT TO DATE GREAT GUYS, YOU HAVE TO STOP AVOIDING THEM!

7/23/24
I feel personally attacked... but also. fair.

First things first: If you want to get to know that cute guy you've had your eye on, you have to walk toward him instead of away from him.

For years, I spent more time hiding from cute guys than actually interacting with them. If I liked a guy, my first instinct was to avoid him. I felt like if we were in the same room, or if we interacted at all, he'd be able to hear my thoughts—he'd know that I liked him.

I was afraid of coming on too strong. If I did try to talk to him, would I come across as desperate? Would it seem like I was trying to pursue him?

I was also pretty convinced that if I did try to talk to the guy I liked that I'd sweat through my t-shirt or say something monumentally embarrassing.

It just seemed like a rejection waiting to happen.

And so, I hid. I avoided the guys I liked, and I prayed that even though I was hiding, they would somehow still be able to find me.

(Needless to say, my dating life didn't go so well during this season.)

I learned a lot of things during that time, but here are just a few of them. First of all, I learned that guys can't hear our thoughts (Praise the Lord!). I learned that smiling and saying hi isn't creepy or "making the first move." It's actually just a thing that regular, friendly people do.

I also learned that, in general, I was able to talk to a cute guy without passing out on the spot, that deodorant works wonders, and that if I thought through what I was going to say in advance, I was far less likely to say something embarrassing.

The biggest thing I learned was that if I wanted to date (and eventually marry!) a great guy, I was going to have to stop hiding from them.

Here's what this looks like in real life:

If you go into a coffee shop and there's a cute guy in the corner, sit at a table near his instead of all the way across the room. If you spot a cute guy at church, sit in the row right in front of him instead of avoiding eye-contact at all costs. If you're hanging out with a group of friends and the guy you like shows up, make a point of standing near him for at least part of the night.

In order for a guy to ask you out, he has to know you exist. Asking him a question, initiating a casual conversation, or just being in close enough proximity to let him notice you is the first step in having a great conversation.

And again, if part of you is wondering, Aren't we supposed to let guys make the first move? then let me assure you that saying hi or sitting near someone isn't the same as pursuing him. It's just a conversation. And you have to have a conversation with the guy before you marry him. That's just how it works.

But I promise you, you can do this. And know that it will get easier with practice.

STEP 2: BREAK THE SOUND BARRIER.

So, you've gathered up enough courage to sit near the cute guy, but how do you start talking to him? Do you just blurt out, "Hi"? Is a full introduction too formal? What do you actually say?

I have some suggestions, but first, let's talk about what you're aiming for here. Right now, your goal isn't to get him to ask you out or to have the best conversation of your life. Right now, your goal is first to get his attention, and second to let him know that you want to talk to him. He needs to know he won't get shut down when he chats with you.

By doing these two things, you're leaping over the biggest hurdles that keep guys from asking girls out.

Hurdle Number One: Guys aren't paying attention.

Very important PSA: Most guys are not constantly scanning the room looking for dates.

So much of the time, the reason that cute guy didn't come and talk to you was because he didn't notice you, which is not the same as him not liking you. He just wasn't paying attention. He was probably scrolling through social media, texting with a friend, or trying to decide what he wanted for lunch, and he was too distracted to notice who was standing right in front of him. (Hint: you!)

But by speaking up, you can immediately get his attention, and that is a huge first step in the right direction.

Hurdle Number Two: Guys are just as nervous to talk to girls as we are to talk to them.

Guys don't want to be rejected either! They have a whole bag of insecurities. They *also* don't want to come on too strong, embarrass themselves, or make a bad impression—just like you and me. That means even if the guy in the coffee shop *did* notice you walk in and did notice you take the table near his, he might still stay silent rather than risk embarrassing himself by talking to a cute girl who might not give him the time of day.

But when you start the conversation, you are showing him that he won't be immediately laughed at or rejected. And that's another huge step.

Now, listen, the way you get his attention and start the conversation does not have to be revolutionary! You're not quoting poetry or confessing your love to a stranger. You don't have to be brilliant, insanely charming, or tell a great joke. In fact, the best thing about the questions I'm going to share with you is that you're able to get his attention and invite him into a conversation without really risking anything.

So, take a look at the list of ideas on the next page, and pick whichever one feels most natural to you! Make any necessary tweaks so that it fits the situation, but don't think too hard about this—you really can't go wrong here.

HOW TO STRIKE UP A CONVERSATION

Ask a general question:

· Do you happen to know what time it is? (This
  question is best used when you're not wearing a
  watch or holding your cell phone.)

· Do you know what time this place closes?

· Excuse me, do you happen to know where we
  order/to check out/the napkins are/I could get a
  church program? This is my first time here.

· Excuse me, is there an outlet under your table?
  Would you mind plugging in my computer cord?

Ask for an opinion or a recommendation:

· Have you ever had their dark roast coffee? Is it
  good?

· I'm stuck between the BLT and the club sandwich.
  Have you ever had either?

· Random question for you: Do you know of any
  good dinner spots around here? (This is the
  question I asked my husband that led to him
  asking me out. I asked him for a good restaurant
  recommendation, and instead of telling me about
  it, he asked if he could take me to it instead!)

Make a comment about something happening around you:

- It is so cold outside! I'm ready for spring!

- Wow! It's really crowded here!

- This place is really cool! Has it been open for a long time?

Comment on what he's wearing, holding, working on, or reading:

If he's holding a book:

- I keep seeing that book everywhere. What's it about?

- Is that book good? I've been wanting to read it! (Only if it's true though!)

- I'm reading that book right now! How are you liking it so far? (Again, only use this one if you're actually reading the book!)

If he's wearing or carrying something that has a team name on it:

- I have a friend who went to that school. Did you go there?

- Do you go to that school? What year are you?

- Are you from Denver? I have always wanted to go there.

- Are you from Nashville? I went there for a wedding last year and loved it!

If you're striking up a conversation on an app or dating website, ask him a question about something within his profile:

- You're from Austin, right? I went there last year and loved it!

- Okay, I have to ask, what is happening in your profile photo?

- So, your profile says you're a (fill in the blank!), but what does a (fill in the blank) actually do? I've never known!

- I like your profile picture! I'm a big skier too! Where's your favorite place to ski?

- Your profile says you're from Oregon, did you go to school there?

- Your profile says you went to school at Indiana University. This is a long shot, but do you know a guy named _____?

- Where are you in your profile photo? That beach looks incredible!

DON'T FORGET!

Now listen, if he gives you a one-word answer or seems cold or unfriendly after you speak to him, that's okay. You didn't do anything wrong. Remind yourself that you have no reason to be embarrassed, and that you were not rejected. It's not personal. Remember that. He doesn't know enough (or really *anything*) about you to make a personal judgement about you.

My best friend's mom always says, "Nobody is thinking about what your butt looks like in your jeans, because they're too busy thinking about what their butt looks like in their jeans!" If he's not friendly, it has nothing to do with you. He's thinking about something else, or he's in a bad mood, shy, busy, or distracted.

A great conversation won't take place every time, but it's not because you're doing something wrong. He just didn't take the opportunity you gave him, and that's okay. This wasn't your only chance, and he's not the only guy out there!

The more you can practice this, the easier it gets, and the more likely you are to find someone who does take the opportunity you give him and runs with it!

The biggest key here is to remember that you have nothing to lose, but truly everything to gain. After all, amazing conversations and romantic love stories always begin in very ordinary places.

THE FIRST FOUR DATES

O kay, now that we've talked about how to start a conversation, let's talk about what to do next. In this next section, I'm going to give you 32 questions to ask a guy (as well as when to ask them!).

I hope these questions help you get to know the guy across the table, or on the other end of the phone. I hope they help you learn more about him, about his life, his faith, and his personality. I hope they help you start to uncover whether there might be something there between the two of you.

But here's my biggest hope: As you read through these questions, I hope you find yourself thinking, *Okay, this doesn't sound so hard. I can do this!* Because you can.

You are an interesting, kind, fun, smart, wonderful person—a total catch. You have stories to tell, wisdom to share, and a great life that someone would be lucky to share with you.

You can absolutely do this, and my prayer is that as you see these questions, you realize that you've known how to do this all along.

WHY THESE QUESTIONS WORK SO WELL

1. Prepared questions really calm your nerves.

I can be painfully awkward when I'm nervous, but preparation changes everything. It may not change how I feel, but knowing exactly what to say gives my nerves the chance to calm down a little bit. These questions serve as a conversational bridge; they give you something to say until you're able to relax.

2. They take the pressure off both of you.

The truth is, you're not the only one who feels awkward and nervous about this whole interaction. The guy on the other side of the table or on the other end of the phone is nervous too! When you have questions prepared to ask, you're actually making it easier on both of you by giving your conversation a place to start.

3. People love to talk about themselves.

It's so true. We really love to talk about ourselves. In fact, studies show that when we talk about ourselves, it activates the same area in our brain that switches on when we eat great food or spend time with people we love. Isn't that crazy?

So, when you give him a chance to talk about himself, it's scientifically proven that he'll walk away feeling great. Doesn't that take some of the pressure off?

4. These questions will help you get to know your date.

The whole purpose of a first date is to decide if you want to go out on a second date. You don't have to know if you want to marry the guy right away (and that's especially true if you haven't been on a date yet, so take that pressure off of yourself right now!).

With each interaction your goal is to find out more about him, so you can decide if you want to take steps forward in the relationship. These questions and his answers will help you do that. They'll help you learn more about him and what he's looking for in life. They'll help reveal if you two connect, if you have things in common, and ultimately, if you might be a great match for each other.

5. They'll help you figure out if he has the "must-haves" you're looking for.

One of the questions I'm asked more than any other is, "How do I know if he's a Christian, and how do I find out without putting him on the spot?" I know that for so many of us it's really important to date and pursue a future with someone who shares our faith. But that brings us back to the original question, how do we begin to figure that out?

In the list of questions below, I've starred a few simple, easy-to-ask questions that naturally fit into a conversation and will help you find out if he shares your faith.

A quick note on this: If you want to know whether or not his faith is important to him, make sure to mention that your faith is important to you! If he asks you, "What do you have going on this weekend?" and you say something about going to church on Sunday, that's a clear marker to him that you're a person of faith. If he is too, he'll likely jump in and you can talk about it together!

Friend, I'm so excited for you. I truly believe that these questions will help you have the confidence to be yourself in any situation. They'll help you feel more prepared and less nervous as you talk to a guy you like. They'll help you stand out as you chat online, and they'll help the conversations flow on those first few dates. And more than anything, they'll help you have fun. You got this! You can totally do this!

Before you know it, you won't be thinking about the questions at all. You'll be totally caught up in the conversation, getting to know this great new guy, which is exactly where you want to be. But before I share the questions with you, here are three quick things to keep in mind . . .

THREE THINGS TO KEEP IN MIND

#1: MAKE THESE QUESTIONS YOUR OWN!

Don't robotically throw them at him like it's a job interview. Work them into the conversation. You can even use a lead-up story if that makes you feel more comfortable.

Here's an example:

You can say...

"I saw this question on Instagram earlier today, and I really love it. This person asked their followers about the best book they've read lately, and it really got me thinking. What's the best book you've read lately?" (You can replace the underlined portion with any of the questions below!)

You can also initiate a twenty-questions game, or you can shorten it to five or ten if you'd like. You can say, "Hey, let's play twenty questions. I'd love to learn more about you. I can go first!" And then have your first question ready to go.

You can also come right out and ask a question. The most interesting people in the world are people who are interested in other people and again, people love to talk about themselves. It's not just *okay* that you want to learn more about him, it's great! That's the exact reason you're having this interaction in the first place!

#2: KNOW THAT YOU DON'T HAVE TO ASK HIM ALL OF THESE QUESTIONS.

You can pick and choose and skip around as much as you'd like. These questions are a tool to help you, so feel free to use them however works best for you and your situation.

#3: LASTLY, BE PREPARED TO ANSWER THE QUESTIONS YOU'RE ASKING!

The most natural response, especially in the beginning, will be for your date to finish his answer and then say, "What about you?" You don't need to have your lines memorized like a script, but it's a good idea, as you're preparing for the date, to spend some time thinking through how you would answer these questions.

Remember, getting to know him is only half of the date; the other half is about him getting to know you. This is the moment to let your personality really shine.

Okay, did you get nervous right as I said that? I've felt that exact same way. *What do you mean I'm supposed to let my personality shine?* That advice is as unhelpful as, "Just be yourself!" What does that even mean?

But here's how we're going to do this. We're going to make this really easy.

The best conversationalists in the world always show up prepared with a few go-to stories.

They do this in job interviews, at networking events, when meeting new friends, and on dates. Having just a couple of stories from your life that you are comfortable sharing that represent you well will help you walk into any situation with more confidence.

So at the end of each set of questions, I'm going to give you a prompt, and I want you to spend a few minutes thinking of a story you'd want to tell. I'll coach you through it—what details to share and what to focus on, so you can represent yourself the way you want. These are little pieces of your life that you'll be able to offer up on this date so he can get a better sense of who you are (and how wonderful you are!).

Not only that, but you'll learn so much about him from the way he listens, responds to the stories you tell, and asks follow-up questions.

Okay, with those last-minute tips under our belts, are you ready? Here are thirty-two questions that will help you have a great conversation with the guy you like, whether you're talking online, on the phone, or in person on a date.

I've broken the questions up into sections so that you know which questions to ask when. The questions build on themselves and will take you all the way through your fourth date! They'll take you from, "So, what do you do for work?" to truly knowing deep pieces of each other's life stories!

32 QUESTIONS

LEVEL 1: ESTABLISHING QUESTIONS

These questions are basic and introductory, but they help give you some context for who this person is, what they spend their time doing, and where they come from. Whether you're talking at the coffee bar at church, online, or on your first date, this is a great place to start.

1. What do you do for a living?

Follow-up question: How did you get started doing that? Do you like it? Have you always wanted to do that?

2. How long have you lived here in town?

Follow-up: What brought you here? What is your favorite part of living here? There are so many great breweries/coffee shops/parks—do you have a favorite place to hang out?

3. Where are you from originally?

Follow-up: Is that where you grew up? What was it like growing up there?

4. Did you go to college? If so, where? And what did you study?

Follow-up: What made you decide to choose that school and that major?

5. What do you like to do in your free time?*

This is such a great question to help you figure out if he's a person of faith. Because if he is, he might say something like, "I spend time at church," or "I'm in a small group." If he doesn't say those things, when he asks you the same question back ("What do you like to do in your free time?"), be sure to respond with an answer that includes your faith—that's the perfect time to say, "I am involved in my church!" And then you can follow up with, "Do you go to a church around here?"

6. Do you go to a church around here?*

If it's important to you to be with someone who shares your same faith, this is an awesome question to ask up front. By phrasing it this way, he won't feel put on the spot. The question sounds casual, like asking for a restaurant recommendation. At the same time, his answer to this question will help you know if faith is something you have in common.

Note: I've marked several questions with an asterisk. These are some questions that will help you easily and naturally talk about your faith.

YOUR TURN!

One of the best ways to get to know someone is to hear what they're passionate about. So for this story prompt, spend some time thinking through one of your passions that you might want to share with your date! You can tell him about your job, a place where you volunteer, a side hustle you're working on, or a group or club you belong to. The important thing is that you tell him about something that's important to you—something that makes you light up.

By sharing this piece of your heart with him, you're giving him a peek into your life and your personality. You're helping him get to know you better. (Plus, you're showing him one of the reasons you're a total catch!)

Some details you'll want to think through are how you first discovered you're passionate about this thing and what you love about it. Also, try to identify one exciting or meaningful highlight, moment, or story from the last year as it relates to this passion. That will give him a clearer understanding of your passion, and help him appreciate how awesome it is!

Use the space below to think through your answer.

LEVEL 2: ICE-BREAKER QUESTIONS

When you date and get to know someone, you want to know if they're your person, right? You want to cut to the chase, flip to the end of the story—you want to know if this is going to work out. But the only way you can have the deep conversations that will tell you these things is if you first break the ice and establish trust.

You both need to get more comfortable with each other before you ask the deeper questions, and that's exactly what this second set of questions is for.

These questions will help you laugh and have some fun together, and they'll give your personalities a chance to shine.

Once you've talked through these things together and laughed a bit, you'll both feel more ready to talk about deeper, more heart-felt topics.

Are you ready? Here they are!

7. Do you have any pets?

Regardless of his answer, a great follow-up question is to ask him if he's more of a cat person or a dog person. That's sure to spark a lively (and light-hearted) debate.

SECTION 3

8. Are you more of an adventurer or a homebody?

Follow-up: If he's more of an adventurer, ask him where he's traveled, and which places are his favorites!

9. Were you involved in any sports or activities in high school or college? Tell me about them!*

This is another great way to tie in faith. If either of you were involved in church or a high school or college ministry, this is a great opportunity to mention that!

10. What's your favorite movie of all time? And what's your favorite movie you've seen recently?

11. What was your first, or your most embarrassing, screen name or email address?

This question may seem silly or cheesy, but that's the point! Talking about this will make you both laugh and roll your eyes at your younger selves—which will take some of the pressure off and break the ice a little bit. Want to know what my screen name was? You ready for it? SKTRBaby2000. (Inspired by that one year when I took figure skating lessons!)

12. What is your guilty pleasure TV show—something people would never expect you to like?

13. **What's a food, or food combination, you love that you rarely admit you love?**

14. **When you were little, what did you want to be when you grew up?**

15. **What's the best job you've ever had?**

   Follow-up: What's the worst job you've ever had?

16. **Do you have any hidden talents? If so, what are they?**

   Bonus points if he can demonstrate his hidden talent!

17. **If you had to sing karaoke right this second and had no way out of it, what song would you choose?**

YOUR TURN!

We all want to be with someone who genuinely enjoys life and intentionally makes space for fun— and that's true for men too!

For this story prompt, think through something fun you've done recently. It can be an adventure you went on, something new you tried, a trip you took with friends or your family, or simply a great day you had recently.

Talk about your experience and why it was so fun. Your goal here is to show him how you enjoy life, giving him yet another reason to want to spend more time with you!

Use the space below to think through your answer.

LEVEL 3: NEXT STEP QUESTIONS

Now that you've asked the Establishing Questions, and you've had a chance to laugh together and see more of each other's personalities with the Ice-Breaker Questions, you're ready for the Next Step Questions.

This set of questions still isn't too intense or too personal, but it will help take your conversation (and your connection!) one step deeper.

18. Tell me about your family. What are they like?

Follow-up: Who are you closest to in your family?

19. What's the last book that you read and truly loved? Why did you love it?*

This is another great opportunity to talk about faith. Maybe the last book you read and loved was about God in some way—if so, make sure to share that with him. This is a perfect way to continue talking about your faith.

20. What's the best thing about your job, and what's the worst thing about your job?

Follow-up: What does a typical day look like for you?

21. What are your thoughts on _____ (a current event you've been following)?

22. If you could have any job in the world, what would it be?

Follow-up: Why would you choose that job? What about it appeals to you?

23. Tell me about your friends!

Follow-up: Are you the kind of person who has a lot of friends, or who has a few deep friendships?

24. What's the best advice you've ever been given?

YOUR TURN!

There's no better way to see someone's loving heart than to hear them talk about someone they love. For this story prompt, spend some time thinking about a meaningful friendship in your life. Maybe it's with a sibling or with the kid who sat behind you in seventh grade who turned out to be your best friend for life. Maybe your grandma played a big role in your life, and you consider her to be an incredibly special friend to you. Consider what you value so much about this friendship. How has this person impacted you and made you a better person? What do you want your date to know about this special person and the relationship you share?

Use the space below to think through your answer.

LEVEL 4: HEART QUESTIONS

This last set of questions will help you start to get to know each other's hearts, hopes, stories, and dreams for the future. This set of questions will tell you so much more about this person and whether or not he's the kind of person you'd like to move forward with into a relationship.

25. What's one accomplishment you're super proud of?

This is one of my all-time favorite questions. It's hard to talk about our accomplishments because we feel like we're bragging. But it's such a special thing to get to hear what someone is passionate about and proud of!

26. When do you feel most like yourself? Where are you or what are you doing that makes you feel the most like you?

27. What are you looking forward to that's coming up in your life?

28. What's the biggest lesson you've learned lately?

29. How are you different from the person you were in high school?

Follow-up: You can ask the same question about college too!

30. What's a big goal you have for your life?

31. Have you ever had a big turning point in life? If so, tell me about it!*

This is a great moment to share about your faith and to hear about his!

32. What's the best thing about your life these days, and what's the hardest thing about your life these days?

This is my favorite question to ask when I have friends over for dinner. It's open-ended, so it can go so many different ways, but it always leads to a meaningful conversation.

YOUR TURN!

A great way to learn about someone is to hear about their goals. For this story prompt, think through one or two big life dreams or goals that you might want to share with your date. This is a great way for you to show him the kind of person you are, what's most important to you, and which direction you're pursuing for your life. As you talk through your goals together, it'll give you both great insight into whether or not you're aiming for similar things!

Use the space below to think through your answer.

GIVE THEM A TRY!

Friend, go ahead and give these questions a try. I can't wait to hear about the conversations that follow.

One thing to keep in mind is that when you ask these questions, if the conversation still feels stilted and awkward, that might be a good sign that you and this guy aren't hitting it off.

If this happens, don't be discouraged—this is great to know! You can politely finish the conversation, end the date, and move on. Even the dates that don't work out help you gain a clearer picture of what you're looking for in a person, and it's always great practice! The conversation will definitely flow better with different guys in the future. So, jump back in and try again!

Sweet friend, you can do this. You are smart, funny, warm, and kind. You are interesting, fun to be around, and a total, complete catch.

Remember, dating is awkward for everyone—you're not alone in that. But I know these questions will really help.

I can't wait to hear how your story unfolds.

All My Love,

Stephanie

EVERY SINGLE MOMENT

Prayers to Pray as You're Putting Yourself Out There

One of the most powerful things we can do for our dating lives is to invite God into them. The problem is, if you're anything like me, you're not always exactly sure how to do that. That's why, I recently came out with a one hundred-day prayer journal full of powerful prayers we can pray while we're single, dating, and preparing for marriage.

INTRODUCING, EVERY SINGLE MOMENT!

Filled with easy-to-follow prayer prompts, this beautiful 100-day guided journal was designed to help you cover your love life in prayer.

But that's just the beginning. Over the course of 100 days, these prayer prompts will help you heal from the past, grow in the present, and find joy, peace, and purpose in your life right now.

You'll feel connected with God through prayer in a whole new way—leaving you full of joy, alive with hope, and ready for love.

Best of all, when you finish the journal, you'll find yourself with a beautiful time-capsule keepsake of this chapter in your love story, and where God showed up in the midst of it. *Every Single Moment* really is a transformative way of praying for your love life.

On the next several pages, you'll find seven of my favorite prompts from the journal so you can try them out and see if this book would be a helpful resource for you.

You can respond to the prompts within the lines I included, you can pray these prayers out loud, or you can write your responses in a journal of your own. However you decide to use this resource, I'm so excited to see what God does in your life as you open this part of your heart to Him.

So, are you ready? Here's a sneak peek of my 100-day guided prayer journal, *Every Single Moment:*

DAY 1

The more time you spend with someone, the closer you feel to them. Think of a first date or the first time you hung out with a friend. Those first few interactions can definitely feel a bit awkward, but each time you connect with that person, you feel closer and more comfortable with them! This is true with God too.

Practice having an honest conversation with God today. Tell Him how you're doing, what's on your mind, what's going well in your life, and what might not be going so well. Approaching Him in a more conversational and intimate way will help you feel closer to Him, and you'll get to rest in the knowledge that you don't have to carry these things on your own.

DAY 2

Soon you're going to be talking, dreaming, and praying about your future relationships. But before you do that, let's spend some time talking about the past. What does your story look like? Have you dated a lot, a little bit, or not at all? Maybe you've been engaged before or maybe you've never been kissed. Today, spend some time telling God about your relationship history. (And if it feels like you don't have a past, go ahead and tell him that too!)

I know this conversation can be painful or feel awkward, but remember that honesty creates space for intimacy. The more you can share with God, the closer you'll start to feel to Him and the more you'll get to see Him show up in your life.

DAY 3

When you think about the prospect of meeting someone new, going on a first date, and maybe even starting a relationship, does any part of it scare you? Tell God about any fears that come to mind and ask Him for help with them.

EVERY SINGLE MOMENT

DAY 4

Meeting guys is hard, right? Most women have no clue (not one!) where to meet an awesome guy. It just feels so daunting. But the beautiful thing is that you're not in this alone. Pray a bold prayer today and ask God for more opportunities to meet great men. And then (this part is super important), ask God for the courage to run with the opportunities you're given.

DAY 5

The most frustrating thing about dating is that even when you finally muster up the courage to put yourself out there, there are still so many ways it can go awry. You're looking for the person who's your person, and along the way, you find all kinds of people who aren't. After a string of awkward first dates, ghosted text threads, or unrequited crushes (the worst!), discouragement tends to seep in. Spend some time talking with God about any discouragement you may be feeling right now, and then ask Him to re-fill you with the hope and energy you need to keep courageously putting yourself out there. Both the journey and the destination will be worth the perseverance they require.

EVERY SINGLE MOMENT

DAY 6

I have a bold dare for you. Ready? I dare you to write down three reasons why you are a total catch and an incredible person to be in a relationship with. You might feel shy about calling out your own great qualities, but you definitely have some and they're worth noticing and celebrating! After all, you're made in the image of God, and He says that His creation is good.

If your inner critic is particularly loud these days, it may take you a few minutes to think of three things. I've been there before, but stick it out. There are a million things you could write down today. Give yourself the time you need to think of three.

DAY 7

When you look toward the future, what do you hope your life looks like one year from today? What do you want to have accomplished? What kind of community do you hope surrounds you? Where do you want to be in your career, in your relationship with God, in your relationship with yourself? What do you want your love life to look like? Take some time to dream with God, and then, write down one small step you can take today that will start you on your way.

That's the end of the sneak peek of
Every Single Moment, but this is just the beginning!

If you head to
SMayWilsonShop.com/EverySingleMoment
you can pick up a copy of Every Single Moment
and dive into the prayer journal today!

And, as a special gift, I have a discount code just
for you. If you use the promo code TALKTOGUYS at
checkout, you'll get 15% off your order!

A GREAT NEXT STEP

**Double Your Dating Prospects: A step-by-step plan
to help you put yourself out there**

If your dating prospects feel impossibly limited
these days . . .

If all the great guys you know are related to you,
married to your best friend, or just not your type
(no matter how much you wish they were) . . .

If you know you need to be putting yourself out
there, but you have no idea how to do that . . .

Or, if you think you know how to put yourself out
there, but actually doing it is another story . . .

. . . then this online course is for you.

Find out more at DoubleYourDatingProspects.com

Also by Stephanie May Wilson

The Between Places
100 Days to Trusting God
when you Don't Know What's Next

Every Single Moment
100 Powerful Prayers to Savor the Present
& Prepare for The Future

Love Your Single Life
Transform Your Season of Waiting into a Season
of Passion, Purpose, and Preparation
- An Online Course -

Double Your Dating Prospects
A Step-by-Step Plan to Help You Put Yourself Out There
- An Online Course -

The Lipstick Gospel
A Story About Finding God in Heartbreak, the Sistine Chapel,
and the Perfect Cappuccino

The Lipstick Gospel Devotional
90 Days of Saying Yes to a God Who Is
Anything But Boring

Available at StephanieMayWilson.com.

ABOUT THE AUTHOR

Stephanie May Wilson is an author, a podcaster, a speaker, and the go-to guide for women in their 20s and 30s as they navigate their most important relationships. Through her books, courses, and chart-topping podcast, Girls Night with Stephanie May Wilson, Stephanie has mentored more than one million women as they cultivate healthy, thriving relationships with God, their friends, their significant others, and with themselves.

Stephanie's writing has been featured on NBC, the Anthropologie blog, and Relevant Magazine. She has also been a long-time blog contributor for CNBC's Nightly Business Report, Darling Magazine, and the Christian Mingle blog.

When she's not writing, speaking, or recording a podcast episode, you can find Stephanie packing for a global adventure with her husband, Carl, laughing with her close tribe of girlfriends, or snuggled up in yoga pants in her Nashville home.

For more from Stephanie, you can follow her on Instagram (@SMayWilson) or visit her website, StephanieMayWilson.com

Made in the USA
Columbia, SC
31 October 2020